ADULT LITERACY
WORKBOOK

Anyone Can Read, Write and Speak Better

D1712930

Copyright © 2024 by Godwin Essang.
All rights reserved.

Table of Contents

Introduction

Section 1: Foundational Reading Skills
Activity 1 - 6

Section 2: Phonemic Awareness 1
Activity 7 - 9

Section 3: Phonemic Awareness 2
Blending, Segmenting, Deleting, and Adding Sounds
Activity 10 -24

Section 4: Phonemic Awareness 3
Activity 25 -29

Section 5: Identification of Graphemes with Similar Phonemes
Activity 30 -39

Section 6: Reading Challenge

Phonemic Awareness and Grapheme Identification
Activity: 20 Reading Passages

Conclusion

Additional Resources

Citations

Introduction

This workbook is specially made for adults who are taking their first steps into the world of reading. We get it, learning to read as a grown-up can feel like a mountain to climb, but trust me, with a bit of grit, lots of practice, and the right tools (that is where we come in!), you will be conquering that mountain in no time. We have packed this workbook with exercises that will help you nail the basics, from figuring out those tricky letter sounds to putting them together to make words and sentences.

Who is This Book For?

• **Adults who missed out on schooling:** If life threw you a curveball and you could not get much formal education, this book got your back.

- **Folks wanting to read everyday stuff:** Tired of struggling with menus, road signs, or instruction manuals? We will help you crack that code.

- **Anyone looking to level up in life**: Let us face it, better reading skills can open doors, at work, in your community, or just for your own satisfaction.

What You will Learn

- **Reading Basics:** We will start with letter recognition and work our way up to reading simple sentences. Baby steps, right?

- **Spelling and Sound Tricks:** We will show you how to break down words and put them back together, it is like magic, but with letters!

- **Basic Writing Skills:** From forming letters to writing simple words and sentences.

- **Spelling and Phonics:** Understanding how to blend, segment, and manipulate sounds to build reading fluency.

How to Use This Book (For Teachers)

The Big Picture

Alright, fellow literacy champions! This workbook is your secret weapon for helping adult learners crack the reading code. Your mission, should you choose to accept it (and we hope you do!), is to be their guide, cheerleader, and support system as they work through these pages. We have thrown in a mix of exercises to keep things interesting and to hit different learning styles.

Making the Most of It

• First Things First: Before diving in, use our handy assessment to figure out where your learner is starting from. It is like a roadmap; you get to know where you are to figure out where you are going.

• **Building Blocks:** We have set this up so each section builds on the last. Start with the basics (you know, letters and sounds) before tackling the bigger stuff. Make sure they have got one section down pat before moving on.

Tips:
• **Show and Tell:** Do not just tell them how to do something – show them! If you're teaching how to sound out "cat," do it yourself first. /c/ /a/ /t/ – see? Easy!

• **Practice Makes Perfect:** Give them plenty of chances to practise. Reading is like riding a bike, the more you do it, the better you get.

• **Feedback is Your Friend:** Keep it positive but honest. Celebrate the wins (even the small ones!) and gently point out areas for improvement.

Keep It Real: Try to connect the exercises to their everyday life. Reading a recipe or a bus schedule might be more exciting than some random text.

Section One

Foundational Reading Skills

Alphabet Review

Objective: To review letter recognition.

Activity 1: Letter Recognition

Instructions: Write the missing small letters:

A__   Bb   Cc   D__   Ee

F__   G__   Hh   I__   Jj

K__   Ll   M   N__   Oo

P__   Qq   R__   Ss   T__

U__   Vv   W__Xx   Yy   Zz

Activity 2: Letter Recognition

Instructions: Fill the empty spaces with the right letter cases:

Example:

A D G M B - a d g m b

Your turn:

F U C L V - _ _ _ _ _

_ _ _ _ _ - s t r h e

Z K Q I O - _ _ _ _ _

_ _ _ _ _ - Y W P N J

Activity 3: Coding and Decoding 1

Instructions: Look carefully. We are assigning codes to all the letters and then unveil them as words. Follow the examples.

a	c	p	o	s	e	u	f	t
1	2	3	4	5	6	7	8	9

Code	-	Decode	Decode	-	Code
943	-	top	fast	-	8159
819	-	___	fuse	-	___
619	-	___	post	-	___
219	-	___	past	-	___
213	-	___	safe	-	___
566	-	___	case	-	___

Activity 4: Word Puzzle

Instructions: The words we decoded in activity three (3) are used in the puzzle below. Follow the example to line out any of them that you can find.

f	s	p	t	l	n	o	i
s	p	a	s	t	i	t	c
p	e	n	f	p	a	v	e
t	s	a	f	e	t	s	e
p	o	s	t	u	a	o	k
o	i	e	a	c	s	s	p
n	r	e	p	t	g	e	t

Write down ten words you can find from the puzzle:

1. _____   6. _____

2. _____   7. _____

3. _____   8. _____

4. _____   9. _____

5. _____   10. _____

Activity 4: Word Puzzle

Instructions: Look carefully. We are assigning codes to all the letters. You will unveil the codes as words in the boxes provided. If you unveil the codes correctly, you will have the name of the objects above them.

Examples.

a	c	p	o	s	e	u	g	r	n	i	m	d	t	f	j
1	2	3	4	5	6	7	8	10	11	12	13	14	15	16	17

The first one is done for you.

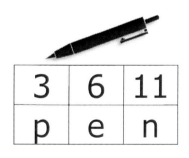

3	6	11
p	e	n

10	1	15
r	a	t

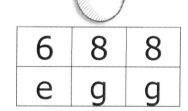

6	8	8
e	g	g

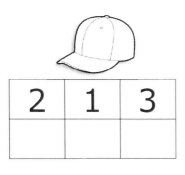

2	1	3

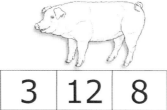

3	12	8

2	1	10

3	4	15

5	7	11

14	4	8

13	1	11

17	7	8

16	1	11

Activity 6: Common letters

Instructions: Circle the letter(s) that can be found in the names of the objects connected to the letter boxes.

Follow the example:

Section Two

Phonemic Awareness 1
Letter sounds

Objective: To develop phonemic awareness and phonics skills

Activity 7: Identification of letter sounds

Instructions: circle the first sound you hear when pronouncing the names of following objects.

- g p v a u

 - r b f h

 - h r m t q

 - c d s t o

Activity 8: Identification of letter sounds

Instructions: What sound is missing? If you
find it, write it in the empty space.
(Hint: f, h, n, d, k, m, a, g, r, o, e).

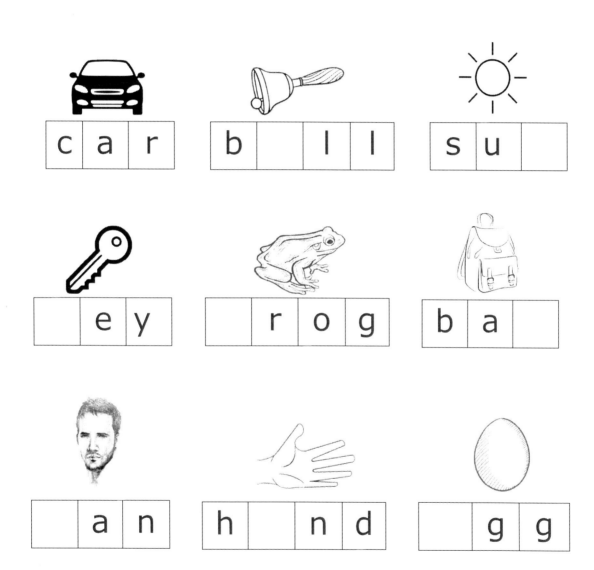

| c | a | r |

| b | | l | l |

| s | u | |

| | e | y |

| | r | o | g |

| b | a | |

| | a | n |

| h | | n | d |

| | g | g |

Activity 9

Instructions: Match the objects with their correct names.

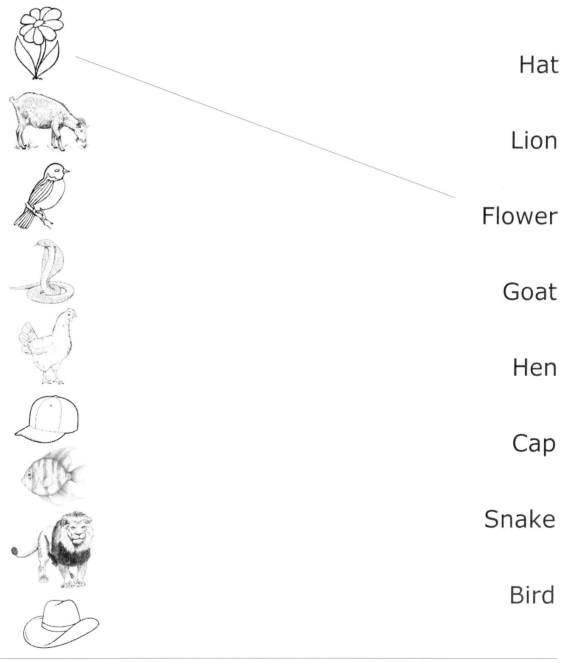

Hat

Lion

Flower

Goat

Hen

Cap

Snake

Bird

Section Three

Phonemic Awareness 2

Objective

To develop phonemic awareness and phonics skills through activities that involve blending, segmenting, deleting, and adding sounds in words.

Note: We are treating the sounds in groups. To learn more about letter sounds, see page

___

Activity 10

Sounds (Group 1):

/p/, /i/, /t/, /s/, /m/, /a/

Words from sounds:

p - pit

i - is

t - tap

s - sit

m - map

a - at

Instruction: the above sounds are used below to make words. But in each of the words, there is a missing sound. Find the missing sound and write it in the empty box.

(**Hint:** p, i, t, s, m, a)

Meaning of words		Words		
A flat piece of material often on the floor:		m		t
Past tense of sit:		s	a	

A gentle touch or tap on something or someone:

	a	t

To take a small quick drink of liquid:

s		p

A small piece of advice on how to do something:

	a	t

Activity 11

Sounds (Group 2):

/b/, /e/, /t/, /n/, /r/, /d/

Words from sounds:

b - bet

n - net

t - ten

r - red

e - end

d - den

(**Hint:** b, e, t, n, r, d)

Meaning of words	Words
To ask earnestly for something:		b		g	
Plural form of man:		m	e		
Something that has not been used before:			e	w	
Furniture use for sleep rest:		b		n	
A name of a man:			e	n	

Activity 12

Sounds (Group 3):

/c/, /o/, /d/, /g/, /l/

Words from sounds:

c - cop

d - dog

g - god

l - log

(**Hint:** c, o, d, g, l)

Meaning of words	**Words**

Past tense of get:

	o	t

Part of the human body:

	e	g

Opposite of new:

o		d

To make a hole on
Something using a tool:

d	i	

Large amount of something:

l		t

Activity 13

Sounds (Group 4):

/f/, /u/, /n/, /s/, /h/

Words from sounds:

f - fun

s - sun

h - has

Meaning of words	Words

Moving swiftly on foot by taking quick steps:

r		n

A person who supports or admire something:

f	a	

Tiny grains of rock Found on the ground:

s	a		d

Physical or emotional pain:

h		r	t

An informal word for love Or sweetheart:

h		n

Activity 14

Sounds (Group 5):

/k/, /j/, /w/, /y/

Words from sounds:

k - keep

j - god

w - log

y - yet

(**Hint:** k, j, w, y)

Meaning of words	**Words**

A tool use to open or
close a door:

	e	y

A feeling of great happiness:

i	o	

Covered with liquid:

	e	t

A person spoken to:

	o	u

A space above the earth
where there is cloud:

s		y

Activity 15

Sounds (Group 6):

/x/ , /v/ , /z/ , /q/

Words from sounds:

x - ox

v - vet

z - zip

q - quick

(Hint: x, v, z, q)

Meaning of words   ## Words

A container for storing things:

b	o	

To stop doing something:

	u	i	t

A vehicle with large cargo space:

	a	n

A fastener for closing and opening bags or clothing:

	i	p

A place where animals are kept:

	o	o

Activity 16

Sounds (Group 7):

Note: we are using normal letters to represent the sound instead. For example, instead of using "/ʃ/" to represent the sound of "sh", we use the normal "sh". We are doing the same thing to any other sound in a similar situation.

/sh/, /ch/, /ng/, /nk/

Words from sounds:

sh - shop

ch - cheap

ng - long

nk - drink

(**Hint:** sh, ch, ng, nk)

Meaning of words

Words

To feel nervous or timid:

s	h	y

A type of colour:

p	i		

A place where goods
and services are sold:

		o	p

To cut something into
smaller pieces:

		o	p

An organ in the human
body used for breathing:

l	u		

Activity 17

Sounds (Group 8):

/er/,   /ow/, /oi/, /ou/

Words from sounds:

er - water

ow - town

oi - boil

ou - loud

(**Hint:** er, ow, oi, ou)

Meaning of words   Words

Liquid derived from plants
petroleum or animals:

		l

A pronoun used to refer
to a female:

h		

To leave a place or to finish:

		t

A person who makes
public announcement:

c	r		

To bring oneself down
as sign of respect:

b		

Activity 18

Sounds (Group 9):

/oa/, /ai/, /ar/, /ea/

Words from sounds:

oa - boat

ai - pain

ar - car

ea - meat

(**Hint:** ar, oa, ai, ea)

Meaning of words   Words

A place where drinks and
food is served:

b		

Something carried as
goods or cargo:

l			d

To take food into the
body through the mouth:

		t

Water droplet falling
from the sky:

r			n

A domestic animal:

g			t

Activity 19

Sounds (Group 10):

/ee/, /ir/, /ie/, /oo/

Words from sounds:

oo - book

ee - keep

ir - girl

ie - lie

(**Hint:** oo, ee, ir, ie)

Meaning of words	Words

A piece of cloth worn around the neck by men:

t		

An animal with wings, feathers and two legs:

b			d

An insert that produces honey:

b		

To stare at something:

l			k

To come in contact with somebody:

m			t

Activity 20

Sounds (Group 11):

/or/, /ur/, /ph/, /th/,

Words from sounds:

or - lord

ur - nurse

ph - phone

th - then

(**Hint:** or, ur, ph, th)

Meaning of words

Words

An image captured
by camera:

		o	t	o

A utensil used for
Eating food:

f			k

The opposite of "us":

		e	m

Meat gotten from pig:

p			k

To set something on
fire:

b			n

Activity 21

Sounds (Group 11):

bl, cl, sl, pl, fl

Words from sounds:

bl - blue

cl - close

sl - sleep

pl - please

fl - flag

(**Hint:** bl, cl, sl, pl, fl)

Meaning of words   Words

Moving in a lower
speed or rate:

		o	w

The surface of
a room:

		o	o	r

A type of colour:

		a	c	k

A piece of land or area
of ground:

		o	t

To strike the palms of
the hands together:

		a	p

Activity 22

Sounds (Group 12):

tr, pr, dr, cr, fr

Words from sounds:

cr - cry

dr - drugs

fr - free

tr - tree

gr - group

(**Hint:** cr, dr, fr, tr, gr)

Meaning of words

Words

To cook food in a
hot oil:

		y

To shed tear because
of pain or joy:

		y

To increase in size
or amount:

		o	w

A journey:

		i	p

Free from liquid or
absence of liquid:

		y

Activity 23

Sounds (Group 13):

"scr, spl, spr, str"

Words from sounds:

scr - scrap

spr - spring

str - string

spl - splash

(**Hint:** scr, spr, str, spl)

Meaning of words Words

Used to describe
hard things:

			o	n	g

To divide into
different parts:

				i	t

A part of a phone
or TV that display
things:

			e	e	n

To scatter or
dispense something:

				a	y

Activity 24

Sounds (Group 14):

ght, air, ure, ear

Words from sounds:

ght - right

air - fair

ure - pure

ear - near

(**Hint:** igh, air, ure, ear)

Meaning of words	Words

To restore health or
or treat sickness:

c			

A word used to address
someone you love or
cherished:

d			

A source of illumination
such as sun or lamp:

l	i			

To perceive sound:

h			

The growth on human
head or body:

h			

Phonemic Awareness 3

Objective: To develop spelling and pronunciation skills

Activity 25: Phoneme Blending

Blending involves putting individual sounds together to form a word.

Instructions: rearrange the letters provided to get the correct name of any of the objects and link the answer to the right object. Look at the example.

gfro - <u>Frog</u>

aanabn - _____

nmawo - _____

ltaep   - _____

 ihsf   - _____

eter   - _____

(B)

ohse - _____

wpaapw - _____

poson - _____

kolcc - _____

drib - _____

rahic - _____

nilo - _____

Activity 26: Phoneme Isolation

Segmenting is the ability to break a word into its individual sounds.

Instructions: Read the words provided loud. Pay attention to the number of sounds in each word. Separate each sound using forward slashes and indicate the number of sounds found. Follow the example blow:

Word	Sound	No. of sound
law	/l/, /aw/	2
phone	/ph/, /o/, /n/	3
bag		
road		
free		
apple		

bird

ate

meat

hope

shop

bite

book

hair

god

vote

open

come

town

Activity 27: Phoneme Deletion

Phoneme deletion involves removing a sound from a word to form a new word.

Instructions: Remove a sound from each of the words to have a new meaningful word.

Word	Deleted sound	New word
ate	e	at
stop	s	top
hand		
play		
away		
farm		

driver

skill

now

plane

there

bring

spend

note

went

good

Activity 28: Phoneme Addition

Phoneme addition involves adding a sound to a word to form a new word.

Instructions: Add a sound to the word to have a new meaningful word.

Word	Added sound	New word
word	s	sword
very	e	every
hot		
need		
late		
aid		

can

one

me

go

see

up

ate

eat

are

like

Activity 29: Phoneme Substitution

phonemes substitution involves changing one sound to another in a word.

Instructions: Substitute one sound for another to make a new word. For example, the /h/ in "hat" can be changed to /b/ to get "bat". Now do the following.

load   - l →   r →   road

rice   - c →   s →   rise

shops -   →   →

part   -   →   →

year   -   →   →

meal   -   →   →

drank - → →

came - → →

fall - → →

read - → →

look - → →

love - → →

smart - → →

planes - → →

pest - → →

gave - → →

Section Five

Identification of Grapheme with Similar Phonemes

Objective: To develop phonemic awareness and identify graphemes (letters) with similar sounds

Activity 30: Identification of letter sounds

Instructions: circle the letter that has a similar sound to the one provided. Follow the example given.

/or/	-	air	aw	eo
/j/	-	f	s	dge
/k/	-	c	m	p
/f/	-	u	ph	r

/i/	-	(ee)	or	d
/m/	-	lm	aw	l
/ea/	-	ar	au	y
/igh/	-	are	i	ir
/c/	-	v	s	x
/ck/	-	k	mn	e
/ow/	-	or	ou	u
/wr/	-	ir	ei	r
/g/	-	d	dge	mb
/ee/	-	i	s	a

Activity 31

Instructions: Group these graphemes (letters) based on their phonemes (sounds) similarity.

oa, i, o, igh, c, o_e, k, ck

oa, o, o_e	i, igh,	c, k, ck

f, c, sc, eer, ph, s, ear

our, ai, i, oar, ei, or, a, ey, u

Activity 32

Instructions: Circle the phoneme that does not belong to the group.

ir	er	(wr)	ear
ar	yoo	ui	ew
ee	ay	e	i
aw	or	er	o
ss	sc	ce	qu
t	j	g	dge
qu	k	z	c

Activity 33

Instructions: From the options, circle the common sound among the three words.

seek, meat, field   - (i,) k, m

back, cat, queen   -   k, a, c

rough, phase, fish -   u, r, f

hall, lung, long   -   g, u, l

right, write, wrong -   w, r, t

Jug, Judge, George - j, u, e

sit, cease, circle   - a, i, s

Activity 34

Instructions: Underline the words that do not share similar sound as others in the groups.

walk   <u>drag</u>   lock   plug

Sing   link   mean line

phone   sun   folk   flow

cease   sin   cheer see

pig   lie   cry   bye

this   trees   trust these

and   all   up   us

Activity 35

Instructions: Pick out other word(s) from the words given.

mate   -   ate,   tea

upon   -   _____

treasure   -   _____

wash   -   _____

shell   -   _____

ease   -   _____

because   -   _____

plant   -   _____

cover   -   _____

shows   -   _____

Activity 36

Instructions: Within the block of letters given below there are some meaningful words. Find the words and write them out. Follow the example given.

sr<u>ego</u>m<u>pet</u>a<u>n</u>p -   ego, pet, an

ftshopbndayu - _____

rstrongjtsong - _____

hgwintfunquitw - _____

btgistdteaxoldf - _____

szworkqhotinfr - _____

gmtenofcutraprz - _____

Activity 37

Instructions: Rearrange the following graphemes to form meaning words.

te, d, a   -   date

k, ar, m, t, e   - _____

s, ng, o   - _____

o, ey, m, n   - _____

ee, qu, n   - _____

t, wr, i, e   - _____

or, t, sh   - _____

Activity 38

Instructions: Complete the spelling of the words described below:

A building where people live;   **house**

A place of worship for Christians; ch __ __ch

An object used for drinking water; __ __ass

A sense organ use for hearing; __ __ r

A general name for people in a country; citi __

Past tense of buy; bo __ g __t

The present tense of caught; ca __ __ __

The second month of the year; feb __ __ary

A room where food are prepared; ki __ ch __n

A title for a village head; ch __ __f

Activity 39

Instructions: Rearrange the following words to make complete (meaningful) sentences:

red, apple, is, the - The apple is red.

car, a, I'm, in - _____

sun, very, the, is, hot - _____

your, dresses, I, like - _____

reading, man, a, better, makes - _____

activities are simple, these - _____

wedding, john, Saturday, is - _____

delicious, I, a, had, meal - _____

is, phone, where, my - _____

what, today, eat, you, will - _____

Section Six

Twenty Reading Passage Challenge

No. 1

Going to the Grocery Store

Maria needs to buy food for the week. She makes a list of items: bread, milk, eggs, and fruit. At the store, she finds the bread on the shelf. Next, she goes to the dairy section for milk and eggs. Finally, she picks some apples and bananas. Maria pays for her groceries and goes home to cook.

A Day at Work

John works at a local restaurant. He starts his day at 10 AM. First, he cleans the tables and sets them for lunch. Then, he takes orders from customers. John enjoys talking to people and making them smile. At the end of the day, he helps clean the kitchen. John feels proud of his work.

No. 3

Visiting the Doctor

Lily feels sick and decides to visit the doctor. She calls the clinic to make an appointment. When she arrives, the nurse checks her weight and blood pressure. The doctor asks Lily about her symptoms. After the check-up, the doctor gives her some medicine. Lily feels better after following the doctor's advice.

Cooking Dinner

Tom wants to make dinner for his family. He decides to cook spaghetti. First, he boils water and adds the pasta. While it cooks, he heats the sauce in a pan. When the pasta is ready, he drains it and mixes in the sauce. Tom serves the spaghetti with a side salad. His family loves the meal!

No. 5

Reading a Bus Schedule

Sarah needs to take the bus to her job. She finds the bus schedule at the bus stop. It shows the times for each bus. Sarah sees that the bus comes every 30 minutes. She notes the time of the next bus and waits. When the bus arrives, she gets on and shows her ticket to the driver.

No. 6

Shopping for Clothes

Mike needs new clothes for work. He goes to the mall and looks for a store. Inside, he finds shirts and pants. Mike tries on a blue shirt and black pants. He likes how they fit. After paying at the register, he leaves the store feeling happy with his new clothes.

Planting a Garden

Anna loves flowers, so she decides to plant a garden. She buys seeds for tomatoes, peppers, and flowers. First, she digs holes in the soil. Then, she plants the seeds and waters them. Every day, Anna checks her garden. Soon, she sees small plants growing. Anna is excited to see her garden bloom.

Going to the Library

David wants to read more books, so he visits the library. He gets a library card and learns how to find books. David chooses a mystery novel and a book about history. He sits in a quiet corner and starts reading. David enjoys spending time at the library and learning new things.

No. 9

Making a Budget

Emily wants to save money. She decides to make a budget. First, she writes down her income and expenses. She includes rent, food, and transportation. Emily sees where she can save money. She plans to cook at home more often instead of eating out. Emily feels good about her plan.

No. 10

Attending a Community Event

The community centre is hosting a free event. Maria sees a flyer about it at the store. She decides to go with her friends. At the event, they enjoy music, food, and games. Maria meets new people and has a great time. She is happy to be part of her community.

Riding a Bike

Sarah loves riding her bike. She puts on her helmet and checks her tires. Sarah rides to the park on the bike path. She enjoys feeling the wind in her hair and seeing the trees and flowers. At the park, she locks her bike and goes for a walk. Sarah feels happy and healthy from her bike ride.

Fixing a Leaky Faucet

John's kitchen faucet is leaking. He decides to fix it himself. First, he turns off the water supply. Then, he removes the faucet handle and the cap. John uses a wrench to loosen the packing nut. He replaces the washers and puts everything back together. Finally, he turns the water back on and checks for leaks. The faucet works perfectly!

Applying for a Job

Maria needs a job to support her family. She sees a help wanted sign at a local restaurant. Maria fills out an application with her name, address, and work experience. She lists her skills, such as cooking and customer service. After submitting the application, Maria waits for a call. A few days later, the manager calls and offers her the job. Maria is excited to start her new position.

Voting in an Election

It's election day, and Tom wants to vote. He checks his voter registration card for the polling place. At the school gym, Tom signs in and gets his ballot. He reads each candidate's name and issue carefully. Tom fills in the bubbles next to his choices. He puts the ballot in the machine and receives an "I Voted" sticker. Tom feels proud to participate in the democratic process.

Calling a Friend

Lily misses her friend Maria. She decides to call her. Lily dials Maria's number and waits for her to answer. "Hello?" says Maria. "Hi, Maria! It's Lily. How are you?" They catch up on each other's lives and make plans to meet for coffee. Lily is happy to hear her friend's voice and looks forward to seeing her in person.

Celebrating a Birthday

It's John's birthday, and his family is planning a surprise party. His wife, Sarah, makes a cake and decorates the house with balloons. Their children make cards and practice singing "Happy Birthday." When John arrives home, they yell "Surprise!" He is delighted to see his loved ones and blows out the candles on his cake. John feels loved and appreciated on his special day.

No. 17

Visiting the Post Office

Maria needs to mail a package to her sister. She goes to the post office and waits in line. When it's her turn, she tells the clerk the package's weight and destination. The clerk calculates the postage cost. Maria pays with cash and receives a receipt. She puts the package in the mail slot and leaves, knowing her sister will receive it soon.

Watching the News

John turns on the TV to watch the evening news. The anchor introduces the top stories, including a new law and a weather report. John listens carefully to the information. He learns about a new park opening and a traffic accident to avoid. The news also features a heart-warming story about a local charity. John feels informed about what's happening in his community.

Cleaning the House

It's Saturday, and Sarah decides to clean the house. She starts in the living room, dusting the furniture and vacuuming the carpet. Next, she moves to the kitchen, wiping down the counters and washing the dishes. Sarah mops the floor and takes out the trash. Finally, she makes her bed and puts away her clothes. Sarah is satisfied with her clean house and relaxes for the rest of the day.

Attending a Parent-Teacher Conference

It's parent-teacher conference day at Maria's son's school. She meets with his teacher, Mrs. Smith, to discuss his progress. Mrs. Smith shows Maria her son's work and explains his strengths and areas for improvement. Maria asks questions about how she can support him at home. The teacher provides helpful tips and resources. Maria leaves the conference feeling informed and ready to help her son succeed.

Conclusion

You did it! Give yourself a big pat on the back, you have just levelled up your reading skills! Whether you started this journey to finally understand your kid's homework, to nail that job application, or just to satisfy your curiosity, you have taken a huge step. Be proud of yourself – we certainly are!

What's Next?

• **Keep at it:** Don't let this book gather dust! Flip back through it now and then. The more you practise, the better you will get.

• **Find your tribe:** Learning doesn't stop here. Look for adult reading classes in your area, check out some online tutorials, or join a reading group. Sometimes it's fun (and helpful) to learn with others.

Additional resources

The ABC Of Adult Literacy: A Toolkit For Teaching Reading To Adults
https://amzn.eu/d/15MrKOs

Reference

[1] https://www.barbarabush.org/literacy-resources/

[2] https://www.leslla.org/materials

[3] https://www.teacherspayteachers.com/browse?search=real+world+reading+comprehension

[4] https://www.literacymidsouth.org/adult-tutor-resources

[5] https://wiregrass.libguides.com/c.php?g=1125048&p=8230106

[6] https://readtheory.org/reading-comprehension-worksheets/adult-abe/

[7] https://readingwritinghotline.edu.au/readers/

Made in United States
North Haven, CT
20 February 2025

66095874R00050